RANGERS TRIVIA QUIZ BOOK

500 QUESTIONS ON THE LEGENDS OF IBROX

CHRIS BRADSHAW

ST CYPRIAN BOOKS

ISBN: 978-1-7392137-8-7

CONTENTS

INTRODUCTION

T hink you know about Rangers? Put your knowledge to the test with this collection of quizzes on the legends of Ibrox.

The book covers the whole history of the club, including league and cup glory, memorable European nights, the amazing nine-in-a-row championship run right up to the present day.

The biggest names in Rangers history are present and correct so look out for questions on Ally McCoist, Alfredo Morelos, James Tavernier, Richard Gough, Sandy Jardine, Paul Gascoigne and many, many more.

There are 500 questions in all covering super strikers and golden goalkeepers, midfield maestros and magnificent managers, Champions League adventures and Scottish Cup exploits and much else besides.

Each quiz contains a selection of 20 questions and is either a mixed bag of pot luck testers or is centred on a specific category such as Foreign Stars or Old Firm Classics.

There are easy, medium and hard questions offering something for Rangers novices as well as professors of Ibrox history.

You'll find the answers to each quiz below the bottom of the following quiz. For example, the answers to Quiz 1: Pot Luck, are underneath Quiz 2: Super Strikers. The only exception is Quiz 25: Pot Luck. The answers to these can be found under the Quiz 1 questions.

All records and statistics are accurate up to the start of the 2023/34 season.

We hope you enjoy the Rangers Trivia Quiz Book.

If you do enjoy it, please leave a review wherever you bought the book.

QUESTIONS

QUIZ 1: POT LUCK

1. What is the official motto of Rangers FC?

2. Who are the three former players to have been appointed the permanent manager of Rangers since 2000?

3. Prior to taking the reins at Ibrox, Michael Beale had been the manager at which English club?

4. Who was the only ever present for Rangers during the 2020/21 title-winning campaign?

5. Rangers signed Ianis Hagi from which Belgian club?

6. Which midfielder was Michael Beale's first signing as manager of Rangers?

7. In what country was Rangers legend Richard Gough born?

8. Steven Gerrard left Rangers to take over at which English Premier League club?

9. The first British player to command a £1 million transfer fee later spent the 1987/88 season at Ibrox. Which player?

10. True or false – Rangers were one of the founder members of the Scottish Football League?

11. Who was the last Rangers player to score 30 goals in a single season?

12. Have Rangers won or lost more games against English opposition?

13. Who was the Scottish top flight's leading scorer four seasons out of five between 2005 and 2010?

14. Rangers signed captain Lorenzo Amoruso from which Italian club?

15. Who holds the record for receiving the most red cards in club history?

16. True or false – Walter Smith won all his cup finals while at Rangers by a single goal?

17. Rangers made their European Cup debut in the 1956/57 season against which French side?

18. Who was the first Brazilian to play for Rangers?

19. In what year did Rangers play their first game? a) 1872 b) 1882 c) 1892

20. The longest winless streak in club history was in 2005 and stretched to how many games? a) 10 b) 11 c) 12

Quiz 25: Answers

1. France 2. Paul Gascoigne 3. True 4. Hugh Dallas 5. Ted McMinn 6. Score in a European tie 7. True 8. Neil Simpson 9. Terry Butcher 10. Dick Advocaat 11. Mark Hateley, Ally McCoist and Marco Negri 12. DaMarcus Beasley 13. Oleg Salenko 14. 13 goals 15. St. Johnstone 16. Eleven 17. 200,000 fans 18. Terry Butcher 19. c) 44 games 20. a) 13 players

QUIZ 2: SUPER STRIKERS

1. Who is the club's all-time leading goalscorer?

2. What nationality is the former Gers striker Alfredo Morelos?

3. Which prolific striker scored 138 goals during two spells at Ibrox between 2005 and 2015?

4. The biggest transfer fee paid by Rangers was £12 million in 2000 to secure the services of which striker?

5. Which legend scored 210 goals in all competitions between 1970 and 1985?

6. Who became the oldest player to score for Rangers after netting against Aberdeen in May 2021?

7. Cult hero Nacho Novo joined Rangers from which club?

8. Which Rangers striker from the early 2000s had a brief spell as the manager of Hull City in the English Championship in 2022?

9. Who scored the fastest goal in the history of the club in a 1995 game against Dundee United?

10. That fastest goal was scored how many seconds into the game at Tannadice?

11. Rangers signed Kemar Roofe from which European club?

12. True or false – Ally McCoist scored 28 hat-tricks during his Rangers career?

13. Signed from Rapid Vienna in 2010, who scored 36 goals, winning League and League Cup medals in the process, before joining Everton in 2012?

14. Fashion Sakala was born in which African country?

15. Who holds the record for scoring the most goals for Scotland while a Rangers player?

16. In 2018, who became the first Rangers striker to score a goal in seven consecutive games?

17. In 1990, Rangers signed Mark Hateley from which European club?

18. Who holds the record for the most international goals scored by a player who has played for Rangers?

19. Who holds the club record for scoring the most goals in all competitions in a single season? a) Kris Boyd b) Jim Forrest c) Ally McCoist

20. How many goals did he score to set that record? a) 47 b) 52 c) 57

Quiz 1: Answers

1. Ready 2. Alex McLeish, Ally McCoist and Giovanni Van Bronckhorst 3. QPR 4. Connor Goldson 5. Genk 6. Todd Cantwell 7. Sweden 8. Aston Villa 9. Trevor Francis 10. True 11. Alfredo Morelos 12. Lost 13. Kris Boyd 14. Fiorentina 15. Alfredo Morelos 16. False 17. Nice 18. Moises Emerson 19. a) 1872 20. a) 10 games

QUIZ 3: POT LUCK

1. What are the official colours of Rangers FC?

2. Club anthem 'The Best' was originally a hit for which singer?

3. Who are the two permanent managers to have had more than one spell in the Rangers managerial hotseat?

4. Excluding Michael Beale, who was the last Rangers permanent manager to not win a trophy while at the club?

5. Who scored all five goals in a 5-1 rout of Dundee United in August 1997?

6. Rangers thrashed which team 8-0 in a November 2020 Scottish Premiership encounter?

7. Who scored a hugely controversial goal in a 2023 Scottish Cup tie against Partick Thistle, which led manager Michael Beale to allow the opposition to equalise immediately?

8. Which Italian team did Rangers face in the first ever European Cup Winners' Cup final?

9. In what year did that first Cup Winners' Cup final take place?

10. Which Rangers wide man, who made 169 appearances for the Gers between 1998 and 2003, was given his nickname of *Terry* after a character in the TV drama *Minder*?

11. In 2002, which Rangers great released a cook book called *Love Food*?

12. Who was the last Rangers striker to score more than 30 goals in a season more than once?

13. Striker Andrius Velička was the first player from which country to play for Rangers?

14. In August 1991, Rangers sold which midfielder for a then transfer record fee of £5.5 million?

15. Which French club made that record-breaking signing?

16. In what year did Rangers win their first league championship?

17. Who is the only foreign player to score a hat-trick for Rangers in an Old Firm game?

18. In 1985, the club tied an unwanted record after losing how many games in a row?

19. Rangers set a club record during the 1962/63 season after scoring how many goals in all competitions? a) 147 b) 157 c) 167

20. Which opponent did Rangers face in their first ever game? a) Callander b) Celtic c) Queens Park

Quiz 2: Answers

1. Ally McCoist 2. Colombian 3. Kris Boyd 4. Tore Andre Flo 5. Derek Johnstone 6. Jermaine Defoe 7. Dundee 8. Shota Arveladze 9. Gordon Durie 10. 11 seconds 11. Anderlecht 12. True 13. Nikica Jelavic 14. Zambia 15. Ally McCoist 16. Alfredo Morelos 17. Monaco 18. David Healy for Northern Ireland 19. b) Jim Forrest 20. c) 57 goals

QUIZ 4: MIDFIELD MAESTROS

1. Which all-time great wide man made 541 appearances for the club between 1977 and 1989, scoring 76 goals?

2. Which midfielder was appointed captain in 2000 at the age of just 22?

3. Which Northern Irish midfielder and Rangers stalwart is the most capped British footballer of all time?

4. Which midfielder was involved in each one of Rangers' historic run of nine consecutive league titles in the 1980s and 90s?

5. Immediately prior to joining Rangers, silky Dutch midfielder Ronald de Boer had been with which European powerhouse?

6. Which former Rangers midfielder, who played 115 games for the club, would later go on to captain his country in the 2010 World Cup final?

7. Which club legend was sent off 34 minutes into his debut against Hibs in 1986?

8. *The Hammer* was the nickname of which midfield great?

9. Which midfielder, who played 346 games for Rangers, was Ally McCoist's boot boy when he joined the club?

10. Which Russian winger broke his arm in his first game against Celtic?

11. McGregor is the middle name of which Rangers player who also won 36 caps for England?

12. Which midfield great had a brief spell as the club's interim manager in 2015?

13. Glen Kamara plays international football for which country?

14. Paul Gascoigne scored his first European goal for Rangers against which Romanian team?

15. Who was the first American to play for Rangers?

16. Which wide midfielder scored 10 goals during Rangers' 20/21 Premiership-winning season?

17. Which midfielder made his competitive debut in September 1983, aged just 16 years and 24 days?

18. Which attacking wide man was a member of the Argentina squad that reached the final of the 1990 World Cup?

19. Scottish-born midfielder Scott Arfield played international football for which country? a) Australia b) Canada c) USA

20. What was the nickname of legendary Ger Jim Baxter? a) Big Jim b) Gentle Jim c) Slim Jim

Quiz 3: Answers

1. Royal blue, white and red 2. Tina Turner 3. Jock Wallace and Walter Smith 4. Pedro Caixinha 5. Marco Negri 6. Hamilton 7. Malik Tillman 8. Fiorentina 9. 1961 10. Neil McCann 11. Lorenzo Amoruso 12. Ally McCoist 13. Lithuania 14. Trevor Steven 15. Marseille 16. 1891 17. Johnny Hubbard 18. Four 19. b) 157 goals 20. Callander

QUIZ 5: POT LUCK

1. Who is the only Rangers manager to have a surname that starts with a vowel?

2. Which former Rangers goalkeeper went on to become a racehorse trainer after retiring from football?

3. Rangers secured their historic ninth successive League title in 1997 courtesy of a bullet header from which player?

4. The Gers secured that ninth title in a game against which opponent?

5. True or false – The original Rangers away strip was a white shirt with a six-pointed star on the chest?

6. Which team do Rangers face in the game known as "The Original Glasgow Derby"?

7. What was the name of the noted stadium architect who designed Ibrox?

8. In May 2018, Rangers were involved in a wild 5-5 draw with which team?

9. Who scored the only goal to give Rangers a 1-0 win over Celtic in December 2018, their first Old Firm league win since 2012?

10. Rangers secured their place in the group stages of the 2019/20 Europa League thanks to a 1-0 aggregate win over which Polish team?

11. Whose 91st minute winner at Ibrox secured that Europa League win?

12. Which manager steered Rangers to their first appearance in a European final?

13. Which Glasgow-born striker scored four hat-tricks during the 1986/87 season?

14. In 1994, Rangers paid a record £4 million transfer fee to which club to secure the services of striker Duncan Ferguson?

15. Rangers signed striker Sam Lammers from which Italian club?

16. Who was an unused substitute in every game throughout the 2002/03 treble-winning season?

17. True or false – Rangers hold the record for the most Scottish Cup wins?

18. During the 2014/15 season Rangers tied a club record after drawing how many games in a row?

19. How much did Rangers pay to sign the great Brian Laudrup? a) £1.3 million b) £2.3 million c) £3.3 million

20. Where did Rangers play home games during the first three years of their existence? a) Fleshers Haugh b) Freshers Haugh c) Threshers Haugh

Quiz 4: Answers

1. Davie Cooper 2. Barry Ferguson 3. Steven Davis 4. Ian Ferguson 5. Barcelona 6. Giovanni Van Bronckhorst 7. Graeme Souness 8. Jorg Albertz 9. Ian Durrant 10. Andrei Kanchelskis 11. Trevor Steven 12. Stuart McCall 13. Finland 14. Steaua Bucharest 15. Claudio Reyna 16. Ryan Kent 17. Derek Ferguson 18. Claudio Caniggia 19. b) Canada 20.c) Slim Jim

Quiz 6: Defenders

1. Which legendary defender's 755 appearances in all competitions are the most by a Rangers player?

2. In 2011, which 41-year-old became the oldest outfield player to play in a competitive game for the Gers?

3. Which defender, whose first name and surname start with the same letter, made a club record 65 appearances during the 2007/08 season?

4. Which legendary Ger and sometime club captain was born in Singapore?

5. Who was the captain that lifted the record-equalling ninth consecutive league championship trophy in 1997?

6. Which full back made 674 appearances for Rangers between 1966 and 1982?

7. Who was the first Italian to play for Rangers?

8. Which defender's 19 goals in all competitions were the most by a Rangers player during the 2020/21 season?

9. Big Slim was the nickname of which defender who had two spells at Ibrox between 1982 and 1987 and 1992 until 1994?

10. In 2000, who became the first player in Scottish football to receive a retrospective ban courtesy of TV evidence, after being caught delivering a kung-fu-style kick at Aberdeen's Darren Young?

11. Which English club paid Rangers £9 million in 2008 to secure the services of full back Alan Hutton?

12. Jig was the nickname of which long-serving Rangers defender?

13. Striker Marco Negri suffered a freak eye injury while playing squash with which former Juventus right back?

14. Which Dutch fullback won three league titles, three League Cups and three Scottish Cups between 1998 and 2003?

15. Who was the first Scottish player to sign for a Scottish club for a fee of £1 million?

16. Which Scandinavian defender, who spent the final season of his playing career with Rangers, was the first player to win the English Premier League with two different clubs?

17. Former Rangers defender and Nigeria international Calvin Bassey was born in which European country?

18. In November 2018, which central defender became the oldest player to make his debut for Rangers at the age of 38?

19. Rangers defender Marvin Andrews represented which country at the 2006 World Cup? a) Costa Rica b) Jamaica c) Trinidad and Tobago

20. What was the legendary defender Sandy Jardine's given first name? a) Alexander b) Walter c) William

Quiz 5: Answers

1. Dick Advocaat 2. Lionel Charbonnier 3. Brian Laudrup 4. Dundee United 5. True 6. Queen's Park 7. Archibald Leitch 8. Hibernian 9. Ryan Jack 10. Legia Warsaw 11. Alfredo Morelos 12. Scot Symon 13. Robert Fleck 14. Dundee United 15. Atalanta 16. Allan McGregor 17. False 18. Five 19. b) £2.3 million 20. a) Fleshers Haugh

QUIZ 7: POT LUCK

1. In the late 1970s and early 1980s, Rangers finished outside the top two in the League in how many successive season?

2. In 1998, who succeeded Walter Smith as Rangers' manager?

3. Who is the only player-manager in the club's history?

4. In 2021, Rangers signed a partnership agreement with which German club?

5. In what year did Rangers play their first game at Ibrox?

6. Rangers beat which North Macedonian team 2-0 in Steven Gerrard's first competitive game in charge?

7. Who scored in the 56th minute to give Rangers a historic 2-1 win over Celtic at Parkhead in December 2019?

8. Rangers signed club legend Richard Gough from which English club?

9. Rangers reached the final of the 1966/67 European Cup Winners' Cup, losing 1-0 to which team?

10. In which German city was that 1967 final hosted?

11. Which Aussie defender was an unlikely scorer in the 1999 Champions League qualifier against Parma?

12. When asked to choose his all-time greatest XI, Dutch legend Ruud Gullit included which Rangers player in his selection?

13. Which much-travelled Welsh goalkeeper provided emergency cover late in the historic 96/97 season, keeping a clean sheet in his debut against Celtic at Parkhead?

14. Duncan Ferguson was jailed after head butting which Raith Rovers defender?

15. Who was the only Rangers player to score more than 30 goals in a season during the 1980s?

16. True or false – Kinning Park is a former home ground of Rangers?

17. In 2010, which Rangers star became the oldest player to appear in a competitive international for Scotland?

18. In August 2012, Rangers began their first Scottish Third Division campaign with a visit to which opponent?

19. From May 1960, Rangers went how many games without being involved in a draw? a) 26 b) 36 c) 46

20. In what year did Rangers release a third kit for the first time? a) 1994 b) 1995 c) 1996

Quiz 6: Answers

1. John Greig 2. David Weir 3. Carlos Cuellar 4. Terry Butcher 5. Richard Gough 6. Sandy Jardine 7. Lorenzo Amoruso 8. James Tavernier 9. Dave McPherson 10. Fernando Ricksen 11. Tottenham 12. Lee McCulloch 13. Sergio Porrini 14. Arthur Numan 15. Richard Gough 16. Henning Berg 17. Italy 18. Gareth McAuley 19. c) Trinidad and Tobago 20. c) William

QUIZ 8: GOALKEEPERS

1. *The Goalie* was the nickname of which Rangers legend?

2. Rangers signed Stefan Klos from which European Cup-winning team?

3. Which keeper made 503 appearances in two spells with Rangers from 2001 to 2012 then from 2018 to 2022?

4. Which goalkeeper was the first Rangers player to appear in a game at the finals of the European Championships?

5. Which member of France's 1998 World Cup-winning squad joined Rangers days after the tournament?

6. Which Rangers goalkeeper represented Scotland at cricket as well as football?

7. Who was the first goalkeeper to be named club captain?

8. Which Rangers 'keeper was nicknamed the *Girvan Lighthouse*?

9. Allan McGregor was one of two goalkeepers to appear for Rangers in the league during the 2020/21 championship-winning season. Who was the other?

10. Who was the last goalkeeper to play for Rangers whose first name and surname start with the same letter?

11. Who was in goal for Rangers at the 2008 UEFA Cup Final?

12. Which Dutch keeper made 64 appearances for Rangers in the mid-2000s, winning a Championship and League Cup in the process?

13. Which rugged defender was an emergency goalkeeper during an infamous 1987 game against Celtic?

14. Whose 535 appearances in all competitions are the most by a Rangers goalkeeper?

15. Wes Foderingham left Rangers in 2020 to sign for which English club?

16. Which German goalkeeper from the late 60s and 70s, had a daughter who went on to become the British athletics champion in the 400m?

17. Rangers signed Jack Butland after his contract with which English club expired?

18. In 1986, Rangers set a then British transfer record for a goalkeeper after spending £600,000 on which player?

19. What nationality was 1990s goalkeeper Antti Niemi? a) Finnish b) Norwegian c) Swedish

20. Goalkeeper William Robb holds the record for the most consecutive appearances by a Rangers player. How many successive games did he play? a) 231 b) 241 c) 251

Quiz 7: Answers

1. Seven 2. Dick Advocaat 3. Graeme Souness 4. Hamburg SV 5. 1929 6. FK Shkupi 7. Nikola Katić 8. Tottenham 9. Bayern Munich 10. Nuremburg 11. Tony Vidmar 12. Davie Cooper 13. Andy Dibble 14. Jock McStay 15. Ally McCoist 16. True 17. David Weir 18. Peterhead 19. b) 36 games 20. a) 1994

QUIZ 9: POT LUCK

1. Before taking the reins at Ibrox, Dick Advocaat had been the manager of which Dutch giant?

2. Which celebrity chef played for Rangers as a youth?

3. Which manufacturer has produced the Rangers kit from 2020 to the present day?

4. The *Little General* was the nickname of which Rangers manager?

5. In 1904, Karl Pekarna became the first player from continental Europe to play for Rangers (and any British club, in fact). What country was he from?

6. What was the only trophy Rangers won during Gio van Bronckhorst's short reign as manager?

7. Rangers secured the 2013 Scottish Third Division title following a goalless draw with which opponent?

8. True or false – Ibrox has the largest capacity of any club ground in Scotland?

9. In 1976, Rangers wore a kit with a manufacturer's logo for the first time. Which manufacturer produced it?

10. Which English opponent did Rangers defeat in the second round of the 1992 Champions League?

11. Rangers won both legs of that tie by the same scoreline. Which one?

12. Who opened the scoring after just a couple of minutes to give the Gers the lead in the away leg?

13. Who scored in both legs of the so-called *Battle of Britain*?

14. Rangers just missed out on reaching the 1993 Champions League final, finishing a point behind which eventual winners in the final group stage?

15. Thomas Buffel, who made 86 appearances for Rangers in the mid-2000s, was the first player from which country to play for the club?

16. Who was sent off just six minutes into the 1992 Scottish Cup semi-final against Celtic, a game Rangers went on to win 1-0?

17. Winger Mark Walters, who won three titles with Rangers, joined the club from which English side?

18. Which goalkeeper missed a penalty in a European tie against Maltese minnows Valletta in 1990?

19. Adam Little, who made more than 150 appearances for the club from 1937 through to 1950, was a qualified what? a) dentist b) doctor c) pilot

20. The longest streak in which Rangers have scored at least one goal stretched to how many games? a) 39 b) 49 c) 59 games

Quiz 8: Answers

1. Andy Goram 2. Borussia Dortmund 3. Allan McGregor 4. Chris Woods 5. Lionel Charbonnier 6. Andy Goram 7. Stefan Klos 8. Peter McCloy 9. Jon McLaughlin 10. Steve Simonsen 11. Neil Alexander 12. Ronald Waterreus 13. Graham Roberts 14. Peter McCloy 15. Sheffield United 16. Gerry Neef 17. Crystal Palace 18. Chris Woods 19. a) Finnish 20. b) 241

Quiz 10: Foreign Stars

1. Which overseas star was the captain of the 1998/99 treble-winning team?

2. Rangers signed the great Brian Laudrup from which Italian club?

3. Who was the club's leading goal scorer during the 2022/23 season?

4. Ianis Hagi plays international football for which country?

5. Rangers signed Alfredo Morelos from HJK which is a club in which country?

6. Which defender set up both goals and was named man-of-the-match in a 2-1 Old Firm win in 2019 which gave the Gers their first win at Celtic Park in a decade?

7. Which Dutch striker was sent off in his final appearance for Rangers in a 2004 game against Dunfermline Athletic?

8. *Der Goalie* was the nickname of which legendary import?

9. Miladin was the given first name of which Rangers cult hero who made 124 appearances for the club between 2004 and 2007?

10. Rangers signed Jorg Albertz from which club in 1996? He then rejoined the same club in 2001 after five seasons at Ibrox.

11. Which pair of brothers appeared for the club during the 2003/04 season?

12. Which defender, who won three titles, two League Cups and a Scottish Cup with Rangers, captained Algeria at the 2004 World Cup?

13. Which Rangers stalwart was captain of the Australian team at the 2004 Olympics in Athens?

14. English-born striker Kemar Roofe plays international football for which country?

15. Former Rangers legend Giovanni van Bronckhorst started his playing career with which club?

16. Whose 45 goals for Rangers between 2000 and 2006 are the most for the club by a Danish player?

17. Which deadly finisher scored 36 goals in just 43 appearances after joining the club in 1997?

18. Haris Luckic, who scored 8 goals in 15 appearances during a loan spell from Newcastle United, was the first player from which country to represent Rangers?

19. Legendary Ranger Johnny Hubbard was from which country? a) Australia b) New Zealand c) South Africa

20. Rangers signed Dado Prso on a free transfer just days after he'd appeared in the Champions League final for which team? a) Monaco b) Porto c) Valencia

Quiz 9: Answers

1. PSV Eindhoven 2. Gordon Ramsay 3. Castore 4. Dick Advocaat 5. Austria 6. Scottish Cup 7. Montrose 8. False 9. Umbro 10. Leeds United 11. Rangers 2-1 Leeds 12. Mark Hateley 13. Ally McCoist 14. Marseille 15. Belgium 16. David Robertson 17. Aston Villa 18. Chris Woods 19. b) Doctor 20. c) 59 games

QUIZ 11: POT LUCK

1. Up to the start of the 2023/24 season Rangers had won the top-flight title how many times?

2. What was the first company to appear as a sponsor on the front of the Rangers shirt?

3. *Bomber* was the nickname of which legendary Ranger who made 278 appearances for the club between 1988 and 1996?

4. Before being appointed as assistant to Graeme Souness, Walter Smith had been on the staff at which club?

5. The club set an unwanted record at the end of the 1993/94 season after going how many successive games without scoring?

6. Which Dutch legend was the first signing of the Dick Advocaat era?

7. Signed for £4.5 million, who is the most expensive Scottish player signed by Rangers?

8. US international and 2022/23 Rangers loanee Malik Tillman was born in which European country?

9. Rangers came back from a 2-0 deficit to beat which Portuguese opponent 3-2 in a February 2020 Europa League game at Ibrox?

10. Who netted in the 82nd minute to seal that incredible comeback?

11. Which Ukrainian-born midfielder won championship medals in seven straight seasons in the 1990s in the USSR, Italy and finally, in Scotland with Rangers?

12. Who is the only Rangers striker to have won the European Golden Shoe Award which is given to the continent's most prolific striker?

13. Which Dublin-born striker scored 26 goals in 66 appearances for the club between 2013 and 2015?

14. Which Rangers striker was the Scottish Premiership's top scorer in the 2018/19 season?

15. Rangers have had at least one player whose surname starts with every letter of the alphabet bar one. Which one?

16. In 1917, which British Army officer became the first black player to sign for Rangers?

17. What is the earliest month Rangers have been crowned top-flight champions?

18. The Gers secured the third-flight title in 2014 with a comfortable 3-0 win over which opponent?

19. Who was the first Rangers player to win 50 caps for Scotland? a) Richard Gough b) Ally McCoist c) George Young

20. How many goals did Alfredo Morelos score in his 269 appearances for Rangers in all competitions? a) 104 b) 114 c) 124

Quiz 10: Answers

1. Lorenzo Amoruso 2. Fiorentina 3. Antonio Colak 4. Romania 5. Finland 6. Borna Barišić 7. Michael Mols 8. Stefan Klos 9. Dado Prso 10. Hamburg SV 11. Frank and Ronald De Boer 12. Madjid Bougherra 13. Craig Moore 14. Jamaica 15. Feyenoord 16. Peter Løvenkrands 17. Marco Negri 18. Slovenia 19. c) South Africa 20. a) Monaco

QUIZ 12: OLD FIRM CLASSICS

1. Who has scored the most goals for Rangers in Old Firm games?

2. Have Rangers or Celtic won more league Old Firm clashes throughout their history?

3. Who was the last player to score a hat-trick in a league game against Celtic?

4. Who scored a hat-trick for the Gers in the 1984 League Cup final?

5. Who scored twice in the so-called 'Shame Game' against Celtic in May 1999 which sent the title to Ibrox?

6. Rangers were unbeaten in Old Firm games in 20/21. Who was the last manager prior to Steven Gerrard to go unbeaten against Celtic for an entire season?

7. Which English import scored the only goal as Rangers beat Celtic in the 1999 Scottish Cup final?

8. Who scored a stunning volley from the edge of the box as Rangers cruised to a 5-1 win over Celtic in August 1988?

9. Steven Gerrard was in charge of 11 Old Firm league games during his reign at Ibrox. How many of those games did Rangers win?

10. In what year did Rangers last defeat Celtic in the Scottish Cup final?

11. Which Rangers great scored goals against Celtic in the 2000s, 2010s and 2020s?

12. Rangers reached the 2016 Scottish Cup final after a penalty shootout win over Celtic in the semi-final. Which Celtic striker missed the crucial penalty to send the Gers to Hampden?

13. Which midfielder's first goal for Rangers came three minutes into his Old Firm debut in April 2022?

14. Who was the last player before him to score in his first Old Firm league appearance? (Clue: it was in 2016 by an English player)

15. Which three Rangers players (all English) were sent off in a wild 1991 Scottish Cup clash at Celtic Park?

16. Rangers beat Celtic 1-0 in 2010 courtesy of an injury time winner scored by which American international?

17. In Old Firm matches in all competitions do Celtic or Rangers have more all-time wins?

18. Who was sent off just 67 minutes into his second spell with Rangers after clashing with Stewart Kerr in a 1997 win over Celtic that sent the title to Ibrox?

19. The record attendance at Ibrox was set at a 1939 game against Celtic. How big was that crowd? c) 116,587 b) 117,587 c) 118,587

20. During Walter Smith's first spell at Ibrox Rangers went unbeaten in how many straight games against Celtic? a) seven b) eight c) nine

Quiz 11: Answers

1. 55 times 2. CR Smith 3. John Brown 4. Dundee United 5. Four games 6. Arthur Numan 7. Barry Ferguson 8. Germany 9. Braga 10. Ianis Hagi 11. Alexei Mikhailichenko 12. Ally McCoist 13. Jon Daly 14. Alfredo Morelos 15. X 16. Walter Tull 17. March 18. Airdrieonians 19. c) George Young 20. c) 124 goals

QUIZ 13: POT LUCK

1. Which former Ibrox star was in the starting lineup for Italy in the 2006 World Cup final?

2. Rangers famously signed Mo Johnston from which French club?

3. Rangers trailed which Irish opponent 3-0 in Dick Advocaat's first game in charge, before coming back to win 5-3?

4. That game was played at the home of which English club?

5. *Mr Tickle* was the nickname of which Rangers star?

6. Who was named caretaker manager after Ally McCoist resigned in December 2014 but also resigned months later?

7. Who was controversially substituted before halftime in the 2017/18 Scottish Cup semi-final against Celtic?

8. Who was the captain of the team that won the 1972 European Cup Winners' Cup?

9. True or false – Rangers are the only club in Scotland to have won every domestic trophy?

10. Which Danish manufacturer produced the Rangers kit between 2018 and 2020?

11. In what decade did Rangers make their debut in the UEFA Cup?

12. Which giant did Rangers face in their only appearance in the UEFA European Super Cup?

13. Who was the last Rangers player to score more than 40 goals in a season?

14. Rangers claimed the title on *Helicopter Sunday* in 2005 after beating which team on the final day?

15. The Gers won the title that day as Celtic conceded two late goals to lose to which team?

16. Which Aussie striker scored both those late goals against Celtic to gift the title to Rangers?

17. Rangers legend Steven Davis started his professional career with which English club?

18. What energy company was the first to appear as a sponsor on the back of the Rangers shirt?

19. What was Ally McCoist's given first name? a) Allan b) Alexander c) Alistair

20. The miserly Rangers defence set a club record in 1986 after recording how many consecutive clean sheets? a) 10 b) 11 c) 12

Quiz 12: Answers

1. Ally McCoist 2. Rangers 3. Johnny Hubbard 4. Ally McCoist 5. Neil McCann 6. Dick Advocaat 7. Rod Wallace 8. Ray Wilkins 9. Seven 10. 2002 11. Steven Davis 12. Tom Rogic 13. Aaron Ramsey 14. Joe Garner 15. Terry Hurlock, Mark Walters and Mark Hateley 16. Maurice Edu 17. Rangers 18. Mark Hateley 19. c) 118,587 20. c) Nine

QUIZ 14: MANAGERS

1. Who was appointed manager in November 2022?

2. Which manager steered Rangers to the 2020/21 league title?

3. Who is the longest serving Rangers manager?

4. Who was the club's first foreign manager?

5. Graeme Souness left which Italian club to take the player-manager role at Ibrox in 1986?

6. Which manager led the club to the treble in 1976 and 1978?

7. Who are the three Rangers managers whose first name and surname start with the same letter?

8. How many top-flight titles did Rangers win under the stewardship of Walter Smith?

9. Who was the last manager to lead the club to a Scottish Cup triumph?

10. Who was the club's first English permanent manager?

11. The Gers last won the Scottish League Cup under the stewardship of which manager?

12. Which manager led Rangers to the treble in his first season in charge in 2002/03?

13. Which manager's spell in charge from 1978 to 1983 included two Scottish Cups and two League Cups?

14. Paul Le Guen joined Rangers after having won a hat-trick of French league championships with which club?

15. Which manager's trophy haul between 1954 and 1967 included six League titles, five Scottish Cups and four League Cups?

16. Who was the only manager to lead the club to a top-flight title in the 1980s?

17. Who had two spells as the club's caretaker manager in 2017 and 2018?

18. In terms of days in charge, who is the club's shortest serving manager?

19. How long did that unsuccessful reign last? a) 217 days b) 227 days c) 237 days

20. Up to the start of the 2023/24 season Rangers had had how many permanent managers? a) 17 b) 18 c) 19

Quiz 13: Answers

1. Rino Gattuso 2. Nantes 3. Shelbourne 4. Tranmere Rovers 5. Joe Aribo 6. Kenny McDowall 7. Andy Halliday 8. John Greig 9. True 10. Hummel 11. 1980s 12. Ajax Amsterdam 13. Ally McCoist 14. Hibernian 15. Motherwell 16. Scott McDonald 17. Aston Villa 18. Utilia 19. c) Alistair 20. c) 12 clean sheets

Quiz 15: Pot Luck

1. Paul Gascoigne joined the Gers from which Italian club?

2. What name is shared by a former Rangers defender and the singer who represented the UK at the 1992 Eurovision Song Contest?

3. What was the only domestic trophy Rangers failed to win in Graeme Souness's first season in charge?

4. Who succeeded Dick Advocaat in the Ibrox managerial hot seat?

5. Which English Premier League manager from the 2023/24 season made 68 appearances for the Gers between 2002 and 2004?

6. *El Bufalo* was the nickname of which Rangers star?

7. Ianis Hagi was born in which country?

8. Rangers were routed 6-1 on aggregate by which team in the 2014/15 Scottish Championship playoffs?

9. Which team did Rangers meet in the only Scottish Cup final contested between two teams from outside the top flight?

10. Club legend Terry Butcher joined Rangers from which English club?

11. Whose goal from the halfway line in an October 2020 Europa League game was described by boss Steven Gerrard as "the best goal he has ever witnessed first hand"?

12. He scored that wonder goal against which team?

13. Which manager signed Ally McCoist for Rangers?

14. With 14 league goals, who was the leading scorer in the 2020/21 championship-winning campaign?

15. Three more Rangers players scored 10 or more league goals during the 2020/21 season. Which three?

16. Billy Dodds was signed from, and later rejoined, which club after a four-season spell with Rangers?

17. Who was the only Rangers player to score 30 goals in a season during the 1970s?

18. Rangers paid £4.5 million to which Italian club to secure the services of Cyriel Dessers?

19. The longest run the club has gone without registering a clean sheet stretched to how many games? a) 15 b) 16 c) 17

20. What was the surname of brothers Moses and Peter who co-founded the club in the 19th century? a) McGrath b) McGreal c) McNeil

Quiz 14: Answers

1. Michael Beale 2. Steven Gerrard 3. Bill Struth 4. Dick Advocaat 5. Sampdoria 6. Jock Wallace 7. William Wilton, Scot Symon and William Waddell 8. Ten 9. Giovanni Van Bronckhorst 10. Mark Warburton 11. Walter Smith 12. Alex McLeish 13. John Greig 14. Lyon 15. Scot Symon 16. Graeme Souness 17. Graeme Murty 18. Pedro Caixinha 19. b) 227 days 20. b) 18

Quiz 16: Scottish Cup

1. Which opponent did Rangers defeat to claim the 2022 Scottish Cup?

2. What was the final score in that game?

3. Who opened the scoring for the Gers in the first period of extra time?

4. Who was the only Scot in the starting lineup for Rangers in the 2022 Scottish Cup final?

5. True or false – Ally McCoist never scored a hat-trick for Rangers in the Scottish Cup?

6. Who was the last manager to lead Rangers to back-to-back Scottish Cup triumphs?

7. Who secured his place in club folklore courtesy of a last-minute goal to give the Gers a 3-2 win over Celtic in the 2002 Scottish Cup final?

8. Which club legend won the 2003 Scottish Cup for Rangers, heading home the only goal in a 1-0 win against Dundee?

9. Rangers routed which team 5-1 to claim the 1996 Scottish Cup?

10. Who scored a hat-trick for the Gers during that 5-1 demolition?

11. True or false – Rangers failed to win the Scottish Cup during Graeme Souness's reign at Ibrox?

12. Which team did Rangers defeat in the 2009 Scottish Cup final?

13. What was the score in that 2009 final?

14. Who scored the winning goal in that game?

15. Which first division opponent did Rangers defeat to claim the 2008 Scottish Cup?

16. Who scored the winning goal to give the Gers a 3-2 win in that 2008 final?

17. In what year did Rangers win the Scottish Cup for the first time?

18. Which rival did they defeat to claim that maiden Scottish Cup?

19. Rangers were beaten by which team in their first two appearances in the Scottish Cup final? a) Dumbarton b) Queen's Park c) Vale of Leven

20. Up to the start of the 2023/24 season, how many times had Rangers won the Scottish Cup? a) 32 b) 33 c) 34

Quiz 15: Answers

1.Lazio 2. Michael Ball 3. Scottish Cup 4. Alex McLeish 5. Mikel Arteta 6. Alfredo Morelos 7. Turkey 8. Hearts 9. Hibernian 10. Ipswich Town 11. Kemar Roofe 12. Standard Liege 13. John Greig 14. Kemar Roofe 15. James Tavernier, Alfredo Morelos and Ryan Kent 16. Dundee United 17. Derek Johnstone 18. Cremonese 19. c) 17 games 20. c) McNeil

QUIZ 17: POT LUCK

1. Rangers secured the 2002/03 league championship on goal difference after a 6-1 win over which opponent on the final day of the season?

2. Who was the first foreign player inducted into the Rangers Hall of Fame?

3. Which Watford striker was the first signing of the hugely successful Graeme Souness era?

4. Who succeeded Alex McLeish as the Rangers manager?

5. Rangers paid a fee of £3 million to which club to secure the services of Connor Goldson?

6. James Tavernier and which Wigan Athletic teammate joined Rangers in July 2015?

7. Former Rangers star Gio van Bronckhorst won the Champions League as a player with which club?

8. Rangers returned to the top-flight after winning the 2015/16 Scottish Championship, sealing promotion with a 1-0 home win over which team?

9. Who scored the goal that confirmed the club's promotion?

10. True or false – The Graeme Souness era started with two defeats in his first three games in charge?

11. Which English striker put the finishing touch on an epic 21-pass move to seal a 2-0 Rangers win over Borussia Dortmund in November 1999?

12. Who is the club's all-time leading goal scorer in European games?

13. *Jukebox* was the nickname of which Rangers striker?

14. Which legendary football manager scored 35 goals in 66 appearances for Rangers in the late 1960s?

15. True or false – The newsagent chain *RS McColl* was named after a former Rangers striker named Robert Smyth McColl?

16. Who is the only Rangers player to win the PFA Scotland Players' Player of the Year Award since the foundation of the Scottish Premiership in 2013/14?

17. *Hitting The Mark* was the title of which Rangers star's 2021 autobiography?

18. Allan McGregor left Rangers in 2012 to join which Turkish club?

19.Which of the following is a former home ground of Rangers? a) Burnbank b) Singebank c) Torchbank

20. What is the capacity of Ibrox? a) 50,987 b) 51,987 c) 52,987

Quiz 16: Answers

1. Hearts 2. Rangers 2-0 Hearts 3. Ryan Jack 4. Jon McLaughlin 5. False 6. Walter Smith 7. Peter Løvenkrands 8. Lorenzo Amoruso 9. Hearts 10. Gordon Durie 11. True 12. Falkirk 13. Rangers 1-0 Falkirk 14. Nacho Novo 15. Queen of the South 16. Kris Boyd 17. 1894 18. Celtic 19. c) Vale of Leven 20. c) 34 times

QUIZ 18: ANAGRAMS 1 (CLUB GREATS)

R earrange the letters to make the name of a club legend.

1. Costly Claim

2. Tam Whistler

3. Risk Body

4. Cherry Butter

5. Ravens Chomped

6. Voiced Opera

7. Casual Pie Gong

8. Infernos Cranked

9. A Bridal Run Up

10. Mr Exit Jab

11. Yo Grandma

12. Human Rat Run

13. Burns a Forgery

14. Radiant Run

15. A Gruesomeness

16. Our Zonal Romeos

17. Ay Hi Landlady

18. Noon Havoc

19. Ninjas Add Rye

20. Organise Fun

Quiz 17: Answers

1. Dunfermline Athletic 2. Johnny Hubbard 3. Colin West 4. Paul Le Guen 5. Brighton 6. Martyn Waghorn 7. Barcelona 8. Dumbarton 9. James Tavernier 10. True 11. Rod Wallace 12. Alfredo Morelos 13. Gordon Durie 14. Alex Ferguson 15. True 16. James Tavernier 17. Mark Hateley 18. Besiktas 19. a) Burnbank 20. a) 50,987

QUIZ 19: POT LUCK

1. Who took ownership of the club in November 1988?

2. If all the players to appear for Rangers were listed alphabetically, which midfielder, who had two spells with the club in the 2000s would be first on the list?

3. And which loanee from Amiens in 2021 would be last on the list?

4. Which striker, who appeared for France in the 1998 World Cup final, scored seven goals in his only season with the Gers in 1998/99?

5. True or false – Ianis Hagi is the son of the legendary midfielder Gheorghe Hagi?

6. Rangers defeated which team 4-0 in the final to claim the 2016 Scottish Challenge Cup?

7. Which winger scored the first competitive goal of the Steven Gerrard era in a Europa League qualifier?

8. Which Rangers star was a team captain on the BBC television quiz show *A Question of Sport*?

9. True or false – Rangers were the first club in the world to win their domestic championship 50 times?

10. Rangers defeated which Turkish club 2-1 to reach the 2020 Europa League group stages?

11. Who is the club's all-time leading goal scorer in European Cup / Champions League games?

12. Dariusz Adamczuk was the first player from which country to play for Rangers?

13. Which two Rangers players were sent off during the 2010 League Cup final?

14. Jimmy Nicholl, who had two spells at Ibrox as a player and a third as assistant manager, was born in which country?

15. True or false – Despite a stellar domestic career, John Brown never played for Scotland?

16. Sebastian Rozental was the first player from which South American country to play for Rangers?

17. True or false – No team took more than a point from the Gers during the 2020/21 championship-winning season?

18. Rangers legend Ally McCoist spent the final three seasons of his playing career with which club?

19. What is the club's record league win? a) 9-0 b) 10-0 c) 11-0

20. They achieved that record score in a game against which opponent? a) Dundee b) Hearts c) Hibernian

Quiz 18: Answers

1. Ally McCoist 2. Walter Smith 3. Kris Boyd 4. Terry Butcher 5. Dave McPherson 6. Davie Cooper 7. Paul Gascoigne 8. Fernando Ricksen 9. Brian Laudrup 10. Jim Baxter 11. Andy Goram 12. Arthur Numan 13. Barry Ferguson 14. Ian Durrant 15. Graeme Souness 16. Lorenzo Amoruso 17. Andy Halliday 18. Nacho Novo 19. Sandy Jardine 20. Ian Ferguson

QUIZ 20: GERS IN EUROPE

1. Rangers secured their first European trophy after defeating which Eastern Bloc team in the 1972 Cup Winners' Cup final?

2. Who opened the scoring for the Gers in that 1972 final?

3. Who also scored twice for Rangers in that classic final?

4. The 1972 Cup Winners' Cup final was held at which famous stadium?

5. Rangers reached the 1972 final after beating which European powerhouse in the semi-final?

6. Rangers reached the 2008 UEFA Cup final, losing 2-0 to which team?

7. That 2008 final was hosted at which stadium?

8. Rangers reached the 2008 UEFA Cup Final after beating which Italian team in the semi-final?

9. Which Rangers star was the leading scorer in the 2021/22 Europa League?

10. Which former European Cup winners eliminated Rangers 7-3 on aggregate in the 2023/24 Champions League qualifier?

11. Rangers were beaten on penalties in the 2022 Europa League final by which team?

12. Who scored for Rangers in that 2022 Europa League final?

13. The 2022 Europa League final was hosted in which city?

14. Rangers started the knockout stages of the 2022 Europa League by defeating which German giant 6-4 on aggregate?

15. The Gers beat another former European Cup-winning team in the last 16, defeating which opponent 4-2 on aggregate?

16. Rangers secured their place in the 2022 final by beating which team in the semi-final?

17. Who scored a late winner at Ibrox to give Rangers a 3-2 aggregate victory and send them to the 2022 Europa League final?

18. Which 2023/24 Premier League manager missed the crucial shootout penalty as Rangers defeated PSG to progress in the 2001/02 Champions League?

19. Approximately how many Rangers fans were in the host city for the 2022 Europa League final? a) 50,000 b) 75,000 c) 100,000

20. Who missed the crucial spot kick in the 2022 Europa League final shootout? a) Scott Arfield b) Steven Davis c) Aaron Ramsey

Quiz 19: Answers

1. David Murray 2. Charlie Adam 3. Bongani Zungu 4. Stephane Guivarc'h 5. True 6. Peterhead 7. Jamie Murphy 8. Ally McCoist 9. True 10. Galatasaray 11. Ally McCoist 12. Poland 13. Kevin Thomson and Danny Wilson 14. Canada 15. True 16. Chile 17. True 18. Kilmarnock 19. b) 10-0 20. c) Hibernian

QUIZ 21: POT LUCK

1. Which former Burnley midfielder was Steven Gerrard's first signing as Rangers manager?

2. Striker Jonatan Johansson played international football for which Nordic country?

3. Which Ranger was the top flight's leading goal scorer in the 2010/11 season?

4. Which Rangers manager was the boss at Chinese Super League side Guangzhou R&F before taking the reins at Ibrox?

5. Graeme Souness left Rangers in 1991 to take over at which club?

6. Which manager brought Alfredo Morelos to Ibrox?

7. True or false – Graeme Souness was sent off in the game where he secured his first top-flight title with Rangers?

8. Which future Rangers star was a member of the Leeds United team that won England's top flight in 1991/92?

9. Which Scandinavian's goal against Inter in December 2005 ensured that Rangers became the first Scottish team to reach the group stage of the Champions League?

10. Rangers were involved in the first European tie between two British sides. Which team from the English midlands did they meet in the 1960/61 European Cup Winners' Cup?

11. *LA Confidential* was the title of which Rangers star's autobiography?

12. Which defender did Rangers sign from Auxerre on a free transfer in summer 2004, then sell to Newcastle for £8 million six months later?

13. Who scored 111 goals in 298 appearances for Rangers between 1970 and 1980 before heading south to join Leeds United?

14. Rangers opened their 2020/21 Premiership-winning campaign with a 1-0 away win at which team?

15. Rangers finished the 2020/21 season with how many points?

16. Which striker, who joined the club from St. Gallen and scored 8 goals in 48 appearances in the early 2020s, was only the third player in club history with a surname beginning with the letter I?

17. Which Rangers legend starred alongside Hollywood star Robert Duvall in the 2000 film *A Shot at Glory*?

18. The Rangers side that won the 2002 Scottish League Cup contained just a single Scotsman in the starting XI. Which one?

19. What is the heaviest league defeat in club history? a) 0-8 b) 0-9 c) 0-10

20. Rangers suffered that defeat in a game against which team? a) Aberdeen b) Celtic c) Motherwell

Quiz 20: Answers

1. Dynamo Moscow 2. Colin Stein 3. Willie Johnston 4. Camp Nou, Barcelona 5. Bayern Munich 6. Zenit St. Petersburg 7. City of Manchester (Etihad) Stadium 8. Fiorentina 9. James Tavernier 10. PSV Eindhoven 11. Eintracht Frankfurt 12. Joe Aribo 13. Seville 14. Borussia Dortmund 15. Red Star Belgrade 16. RB Leipzig 17. John Lundstram 18. Mauricio Pochettino 19. c) 100,000 fans 20. c) Aaron Ramsey

QUIZ 22: SCOTTISH LEAGUE CUP

1. Rangers last won the Scottish League Cup in 2011. Which side did they defeat 2-1 AET in the final?

2. Who opened the scoring for the Gers in that 2011 final?

3. Whose strike in extra time secured the win for the light blues?

4. Rangers were involved in the first ever League Cup final, defeating which team 4-0 in the final?

5. In what decade did that inaugural Scottish League Cup take place?

6. True or false – In the first Old Firm League Cup final, Rangers were routed 7-1?

7. Who came off the bench to score an overhead kick which gave Rangers a memorable 1993 League Cup final win over Hibernian?

8. Rangers routed which team 5-1 in the 2005 final?

9. Which Greek defender scored twice in that game?

10. Rangers won the 2002 Scottish League Cup after beating which second-flight team 4-0 in the final?

11. Rangers defeated which team on penalties in the 2008 final after the game was tied at 2-2 after extra time?

12. Who scored the crucial penalty that gave the Gers the trophy?

13. Rangers won the League Cup in 2010 despite having two players sent off in the final against which team?

14. Who headed an 84th minute winner to give the Gers a famous 1-0 victory in that 2010 final?

15. Which English defender was the captain of the Rangers team that beat Aberdeen to win the 1987 League Cup final?

16. True or false – Rangers have won the League Cup more often than any other team?

17. Rangers claimed the 1996 League Cup after a classic 4-3 win over which rival?

18. Two Rangers players scored twice in that final. Ally McCoist was one, who was the other?

19. Who scored the crucial penalty that gave Rangers a shootout win over Aberdeen in the classic 1987 final? a) Ian Durrant b) Robert Fleck c) Ally McCoist

20. Up to the close of the 2022/23 season, how many times had Rangers won the League Cup? a) 26 b) 27 c) 28

Quiz 21: Answers

1. Scott Arfield 2. Finland 3. Kenny Miller 4. Gio van Bronckhorst 5. Liverpool 6. Pedro Caixinha 7. True 8. Rod Wallace 9. Peter Løvenkrands 10. Wolverhampton Wanderers 11. Lorenzo Amoruso 12. Jean-Alain Boumsong 13. Derek Parlane 14. Aberdeen 15. 102 points 16. Cedric Itten 17. Ally McCoist 18. Barry Ferguson 19. a) 0-8 20. b) Celtic

Quiz 23: Pot Luck

1. Rangers have two official crests. One features the overlapping letters RFC. What animal features on the other?

2. Whom did Graeme Souness succeed as Rangers' manager?

3. Which Rangers defender (who was a nephew of Bill Shankly) had a goal disallowed in the 1967 European Cup Winners' Cup final?

4. With 27 goals in all competitions, who was the club's leading scorer in the 1998/99 treble-winning season?

5. Joe Aribo left which London club to join Rangers?

6. Which Rangers star provided the voice of Viktor in the Romanian version of the hit Disney movie *Frankenweenie*?

7. Rangers were shocked in the 2017/18 Europa League qualifiers, losing to minnows Progres Niederkorn, a club from which country?

8. Rangers secured the 2021 Premiership title after Celtic could only manage a 0-0 draw against which team?

9. True or false – Rangers reached the final of the 2008 UEFA Cup despite scoring just five goals in eight games in the knockout rounds?

10. Complete the name of the popular Rangers podcast – *Heart and ...*?

11. Rangers signed Ally McCoist from which English club?

12. How much did they pay to secure the services of their star striker?

13. Orjan Persson, who scored 31 goals in 113 appearances for Rangers, represented which country at the 1970 World Cup?

14. Rangers' closest rivals for the 2020/21 Premiership title finished how many points behind the Gers?

15. Which English side defeated Rangers in the semi-final of the 1968/69 Inter City Fairs Cup?

16. Which central defender, who made 44 appearances for Rangers in the early 1990s, later joined Celtic after spells at Coventry, Dundee United and Hearts?

17. Who were the five Rangers players to score 10 or more league goals during the 2022/23 season?

18. Rangers signed Todd Cantwell from which English club?

19. Rangers legend Richard Gough was raised in which African country? a) Kenya b) South Africa c) Zimbabwe

20. How many goals did Ally McCoist score in Old Firm games? a) 25 b) 26 c) 27

Quiz 22: Answers

1. Celtic 2. Steven Davis 3. Nikica Jelavic 4. Aberdeen 5. 1940s 6. True 7. Ally McCoist 8. Motherwell 9. Sotirios Kyrgiakos 10. Ayr United 11. Dundee United 12. Kris Boyd 13. St. Mirren 14. Kenny Miller 15. Graham Roberts 16. True 17. Hearts 18. Paul Gascoigne 19. a) Ian Durrant 20. b) 27 times

QUIZ 24: ANAGRAMS 2 (MODERN GREATS)

Rearrange the letters to make the name of a player who has appeared for the club since 2020.

1. Rent Yank
2. For Me Korea
3. Cream Roll Gang
4. I Again His
5. Solo Role Framed
6. Jive Term Arenas
7. I Jar Oboe
8. Karma Angel
9. TV Said Seven
10. Barbaric Ions
11. Long Cordon Son
12. Bale Scans Ivy
13. Mr Jan Holds Nut
14. Elf Dictators
15. Alias Hank Oafs
16. Jug Hill Conman
17. Headliner Flip

18. National Cook

19. A Lilt Milkman

20. Vine Based

Quiz 23: Answers

1. A lion 2. Jock Wallace 3. Roger Hynd 4. Rod Wallace 5. Charlton 6. Ianis Hagi 7. Luxembourg 8. Dundee United 9. True 10. Hand 11. Sunderland 12. £185,000 13. Sweden 14. 25 points 15. Newcastle United 16. Steven Pressley 17. Tavernier, Colak, Morelos, Sakala and Tillman 18. Norwich 19. b) South Africa 20. c) 27 goals

Quiz 25: Pot Luck

1. Excluding the UK, which country has provided the most players for Rangers?

2. Who famously 'booked' referee Dougie Smith during a 7-0 rout of Hibs in 1995?

3. True or false – Rangers boss Michael Beale had a spell as the assistant manager of Brazilian giants Sao Paulo?

4. Which referee was hit by a coin thrown by a Celtic fan during a controversial 1999 Old Firm clash?

5. Which colourful Rangers winger from the mid-1980s went on to become the kit man for Derbyshire County Cricket Club after his retirement from football?

6. In a 1956 game at Ibrox, Max Murray became the first Rangers player to do what?

7. True or false – For a time, Rangers wore a blue and white hooped home shirt?

8. Ian Durrant suffered a horrendous injury in a 1989 game against Aberdeen following a terrible challenge from which midfielder?

9. Which club legend was fined £500 after kicking a hole in the referee's dressing room door following that infamous game against Aberdeen?

10. The Gers were beaten in the final of the 2008 UEFA Cup by a team managed by which former Rangers boss?

11. Who were the three Rangers strikers to score more than 30 goals in a season during the 1990s?

12. Which left-sided player, who made 30 appearances for Rangers in the late 2000s, is the only American to have appeared in four World Cups?

13. Which striker, who had a brief spell at Ibrox in the 1995/96 season, scored five goals in a 1994 World Cup game against Cameroon?

14. How many goals did Rangers concede throughout the whole of the 2020/21 Premiership campaign?

15. Rangers' record win in the League Cup was a 9-1 thrashing of which opponent in 1964?

16. How many cup finals did Walter Smith win while at Rangers?

17. Approximately how many Rangers fans gathered in Manchester for the 2008 UEFA Cup final?

18. Who is the only English Rangers player in the Scottish Football Hall of Fame?

19. During the 1992/93 seasons Rangers were unbeaten at home and abroad for how many successive games? a) 42 b) 43 c) 44

20. How many foreign players were involved in Rangers' nine championships in a row? a) 13 b) 15 c) 17

Quiz 24: Answers

1. Ryan Kent 2. Kemar Roofe 3. Allan McGregor 4. Ianis Hagi 5. Alfredo Morelos 6. James Tavernier 7. Joe Aribo 8. Glen Kamara 9. Steven Davis 10. Borna Barisic 11. Connor Goldson 12. Calvin Bassey 13. John Lundstram 14. Scott Arfield 15. Fashion Sakala 16. Jon McLaughlin 17. Filip Helander 18. Antonio Colak 19. Malik Tillman 20. Ben Davies

ACKNOWLEDGEMENTS

Many thanks to designer extraordinaire Graham Nash, Heidi Grant, Bill Rankin, Ken and Veronica Bradshaw, Steph, James, Ben and Will Roe.

ABOUT THE AUTHOR

C hris Bradshaw has written more than 30 quiz book including titles on the NFL, college football, golf, tennis, Formula One, Moto GP and cycling. He has also written on cricket for The Times (of London) as well as on soccer, darts and poker.

ALSO BY CHRIS BRADSHAW

Denver Broncos: Top 5 of Everything – Ranking the Top Players, Greatest
Games, and Wildest Moments in Broncos History

Formula One Trivia Quiz Book

MotoGP Trivia Quiz Book

Golf Trivia Quiz Book

Tennis Trivia Quiz Book

Boston Red Sox Trivia Quiz Book

Chicago Cubs Trivia Quiz Book

New York Yankees Trivia Quiz Book

Baltimore Ravens Trivia Quiz Book

Chicago Bears Trivia Quiz Book

Cincinnati Bengals Trivia Quiz Book

Dallas Cowboys Trivia Quiz Book

Denver Broncos Trivia Quiz Book

Green Bay Packers Trivia Quiz Book

Kansas City Chiefs Trivia Quiz Book

Miami Dolphins Trivia Quiz Book

Minnesota Vikings Trivia Quiz Book

New England Patriots Trivia Quiz Book

New York Giants Trivia Quiz Book

Printed in Great Britain
by Amazon

34718766R00035